Lake Superior, Wawa, Kenora and Dryden, Ontario in Colour Photos, Saving Our History One Photo at a Time

Photography
by Barbara Raué
2017

Series Name:
Cruising Ontario

Book 172: Lake Superior, Wawa, Kenora, Dryden

Cover photo: Tudor style house in Dryden, Page 50

Series Name: Cruising Ontario
Saving Our History One Photo at a Time
in colour photos

Books Available in Alphabetical Order:
Aberfoyle, Acton, Alton, Amherstburg, Ancaster, Arthur, Aylmer, Ayr, Bloomingdale, Brantford, Burlington, Caledon, Caledonia, Cambridge, Clifford, Conestogo, Delhi, Dorchester to Aylmer, Drayton, Drumbo, Dundas, Eden Mills, Elmira, Elora, Essex, Fergus, Guelph, Hagersville, Hamilton, Hanover, Harriston, Hespeler, Jarvis, Kingston, Kingsville, Kitchener, Linwood, Listowel, London, Lucknow, Mono, Mount Forest, Neustadt, New Hamburg, Niagara-on-the-Lake, Oakville, Orangeville, Orillia, Owen Sound, Palmerston, Peterborough, Petrolia, Port Elgin, Preston, Rockwood, Sarnia, Seaforth, Sheffield, Shelburne, Simcoe, Southampton, St. Jacobs, St. Marys, St. Thomas, Stoney Creek, Stratford, Thamesford, Tillsonburg, Waterdown, Waterford, Waterloo, Welland, Wellesley, Windsor, Wingham, Woodstock

Book 140-145: Kingston
Book 146-149: Ottawa
Book 150-151: Midland
Book 152: Penetanguishene
Book 153: Kemptville
Book 154: Cornwall
Book 155: Mariatown to Maitland
Book 156: Morrisburg
Book 157: Brockville
Book 158: Merrickville
Book 159: Smiths Falls
Book 160: Portland, Newboro
Book 161: Westport & Area

Book 162: Perth
Book 163-166: Belleville
Book 167-168: Port Colborne
Book 169: Erin in Colour
Book 170: Goderich in Colour
Book 171: Sault Ste. Marie
Book 172: Lake Superior

Other Books by Barbara Raue

Coins of Gold

Arrows, Indians and Love

The Life and Times of Barbara
Volume 1: Inventions That Have Enhanced My Life
Volume 2: Entertainment That I Have Enjoyed
Volume 3: East Coast Trips
Volume 4: Olympics Have Always Intrigued Me
Volume 5: Wonders of the World
Volume 6: Caribbean Cruises We Have Enjoyed
Volume 7: Animals
Volume 8: Storms and Other Major Disasters in My Lifetime
Volume 9: Wars, Terrorist Attacks and Major Disasters

The Cromwell Family Book

Laura Secord Discovered

Daddy Where Are You?

Montana Series
Book 1: Montana Dream
Book 2: Life on the Montana Frontier
Book 3: Montana to Boston and Back
Book 4: Montana Sons Go to War
Book 5: Montana Sons Return From War

Visit Barbara's website to view all of her books
http://barbararaue.ca

Table of Contents

Lake Superior
- Pancake Bay — Page 8
- Alona Bay — Page 10
- Pinguisibi — Page 15
- Katherine Cove — Page 16
- Old Woman Bay — Page 18
- Wawa — Page 20
- Marathon — Page 33
- Nipigon — Page 34
- North Woods — Page 39

Kenora — Page 41

Dryden — Page 46

Architectural Terms — Page 51

Building Styles — Page 53

Lake Superior is the largest freshwater lake in the world by surface area, and the third largest in volume. If the coast of Lake Superior was unravelled into a highway, it would extend 2,939 kilometers (1826 miles). The deepest spot is 406 meters (1,322 feet). Lake Superior presented many challenges to shipping. As interest in the resources of the north grew, investors wanted a more reliable form of transportation and the Algoma Central Railway was built. It was intended to bring iron ore and pulp logs from Wawa and Hearst to the mills of Sault Ste. Marie. With the completion of the railroad in 1914, loggers, tourists and artists travelled to places that had been difficult to reach.

Before Lake Superior Provincial Park was created, a group of artists came to paint pictures of Canada. J.E.H. Macdonald found a multi-channeled falls which he painted showing the foam, the reflections, the colors and the magic. These artists were experimenting with new techniques that showed the ruggedness and beauty of the land. Each fall between 1918 and 1922, members of the Group of Seven painted the newly accessible landscape of the Algoma region as the railway was built. They lived in a rented boxcar and travelled up and down the railway in a three-wheeled handcart called a velocipede. A canoe took them to locations away from the track. The bold new style of painting used vibrant colors.

The Agawa River Valley formed a natural pathway through the wilderness a section of the railway follows the route through the Agawa Canyon.

When the first Europeans travelled to the Wawa region in the late 1600s, they were introduced to a rugged landscape occupied by the Ojibway people. Wawa means clear water. Somewhere along the way wawa may have been mistranslated to wild goose instead of wewe which means snow goose. The wild goose story stuck and thus was born Wawa's legendary Wawa Goose.

Kenora is a small city situated on the Lake of the Woods in Northwestern Ontario, close to the Manitoba border. It is about two hundred kilometers (124 miles) east of Winnipeg. Kenora's future site was in the territory of the Ojibway when the first European, Jacques de Novon, sighted Lake of the Woods in 1688. Pierre La Verendrye established a French trading post, Fort St. Charles, to the south of present-day Kenora near the current Canada/United States border in 1732, and France maintained the post until 1763 when it lost the territory to the British in the Seven Years' War. In 1836 the Hudson's Bay Company established a post on Old Fort Island, and in 1861, the Company opened a post on the mainland at Kenora's current location.

In 1878, the company surveyed lots for the permanent settlement of *Rat Portage* ("portage to the country of the muskrat") — the community kept that name until 1905, when it was renamed Kenora.

Gold and the railroad were both important in the community's early history: gold was first discovered in the area in 1850, and by 1893, twenty mines were operating within 24 kilometers (15 miles) of the town. The first Canadian ocean-to-ocean train passed through in 1886 on the Canadian Pacific Railway.

A highway was built through Kenora in 1932, becoming part of Canada's first coast-to-coast highway in 1943, and then part of the Trans-Canada Highway. In 1967, the year of the Canadian Centennial, Kenora erected a sculpture known as Husky the Muskie. It has become the town's mascot and one of its most recognizable features.

A dramatic bank robbery took place in Kenora on May 10, 1973. An unknown man entered the Canadian Imperial Bank of Commerce heavily armed. After robbing the bank, the robber was preparing to enter a city vehicle driven by undercover police officer Don Milliard. A sniper positioned across the street shot the robber causing the explosives he was carrying to detonate and kill the robber. Most of the windows on the shops on the main street were shattered as a result of the blast.

The importance of the logging industry declined in the second part of the 20th century, and the last log boom was towed into Kenora in 1985. The tourist and recreation industries have become more important.

Dryden is the second-largest city in the Kenora District of Northwestern Ontario. It is located on Wabigoon Lake.

The Dryden area is part of the Ojibway nation, which covers a large area from Lake Huron in the east to Lake of the Woods and beyond. The Ojibway are nomadic with groups from family to village size moving over the land with the seasons and the availability of game or the necessities of life.

The settlement was founded as an agricultural community by John Dryden, Ontario's Minister of Agriculture in 1895. While his train was stopped at what was then known as Barclay Tank to re-water, he noticed clover growing and decided to found an experimental farm the following year. The farm's success brought settlers from other areas and the community came to be known as New Prospect.

Pulp and paper came to the town in 1910. Today, its main industries are agriculture, tourism and mining. The town was the site of the March 10, 1989 crash of Air Ontario Flight 1363 which killed twenty-four people.

Dryden is known by people passing by as the home of "Max the Moose", Dryden's 5.6 metres (18 foot) high mascot on the Trans-Canada Highway.

Pancake Bay

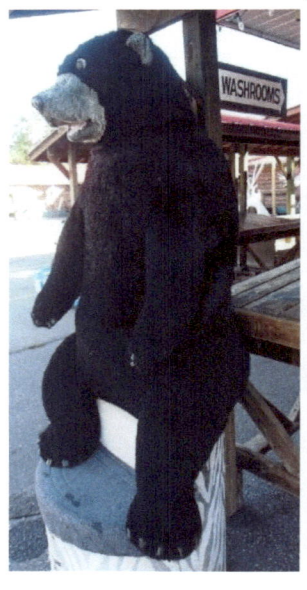
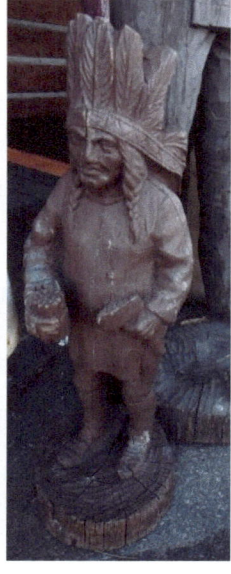
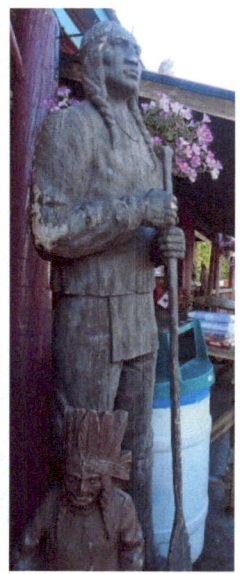
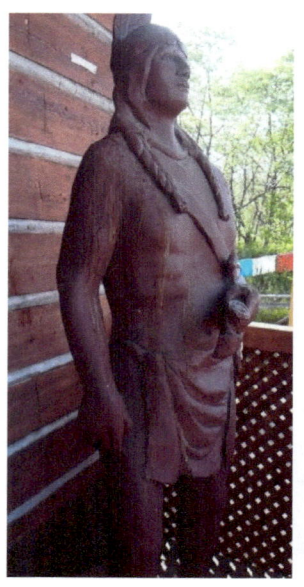
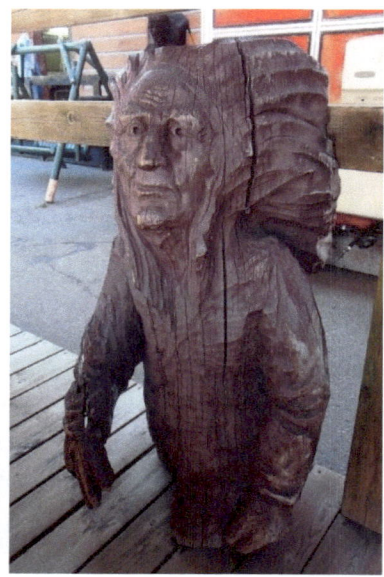

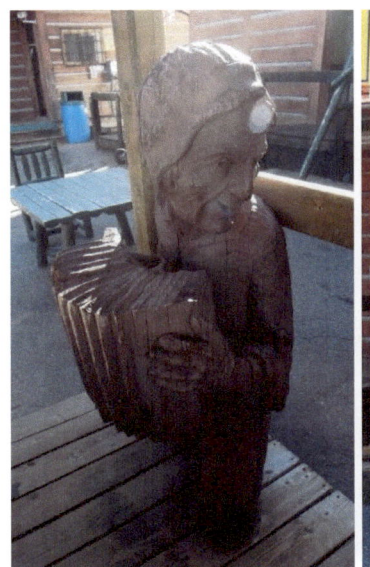
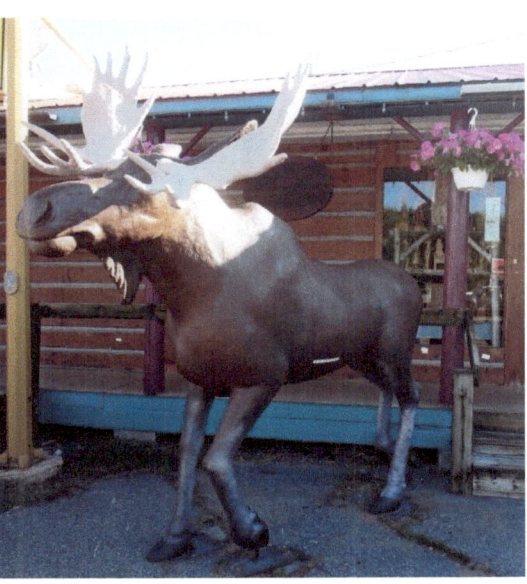
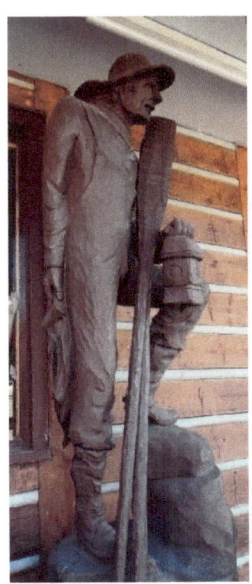
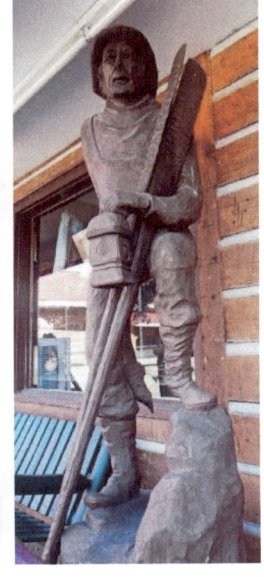

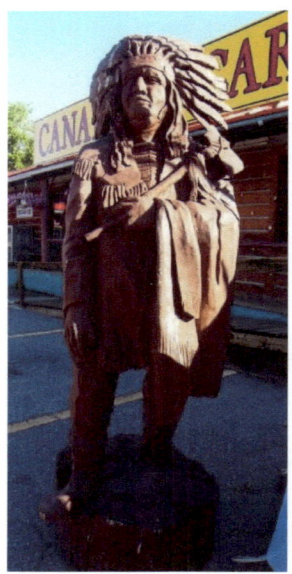 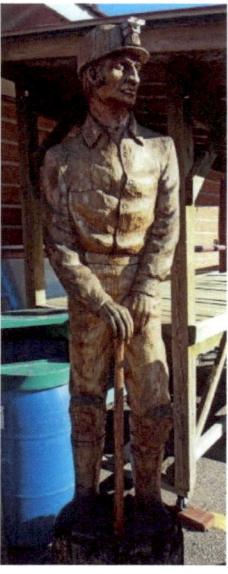

Alona Bay
It has 10% of the world's fresh surface water.

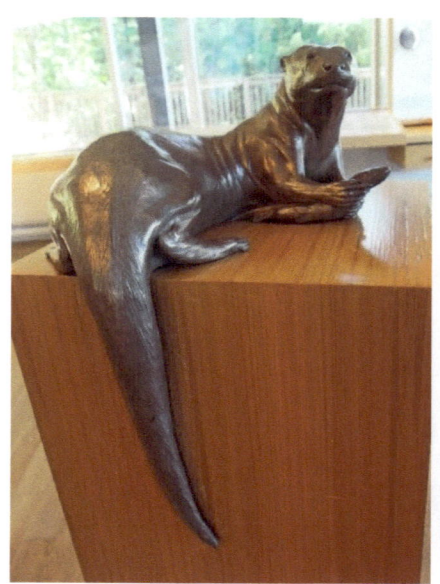 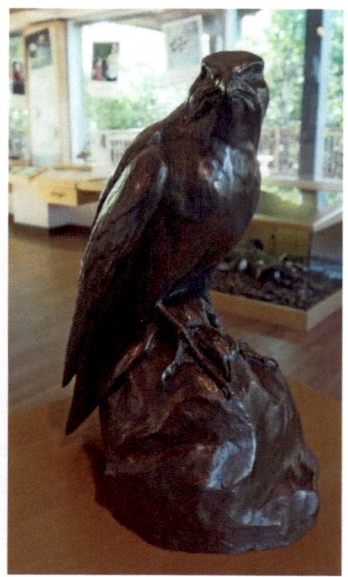

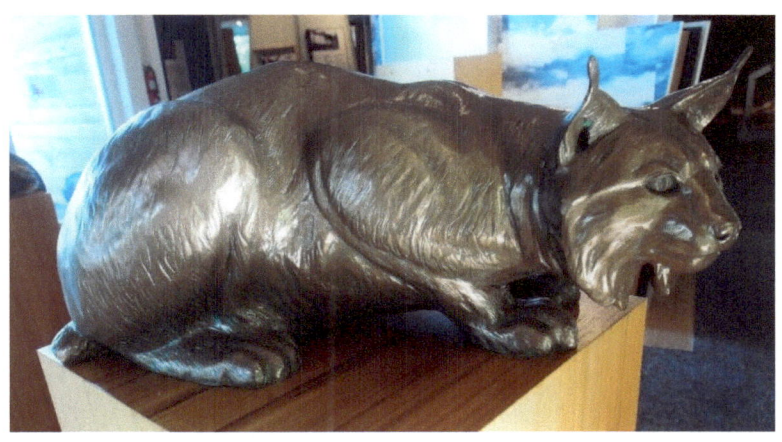

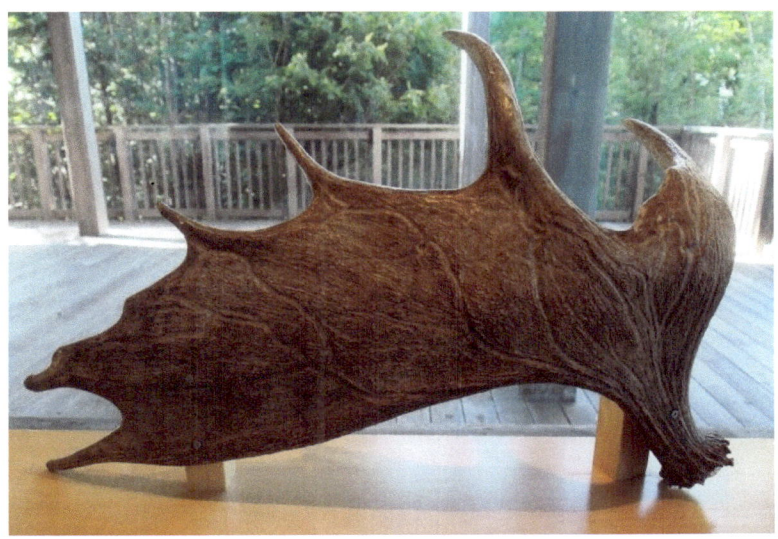

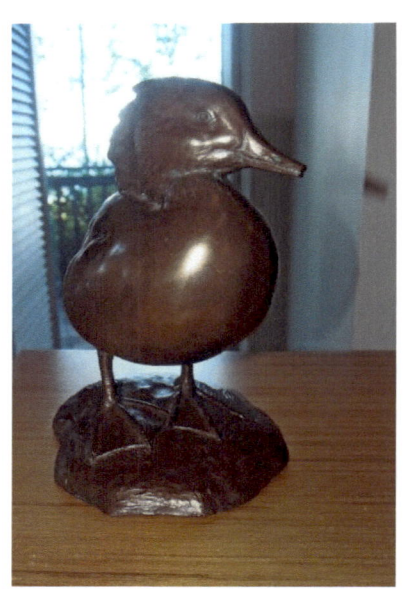

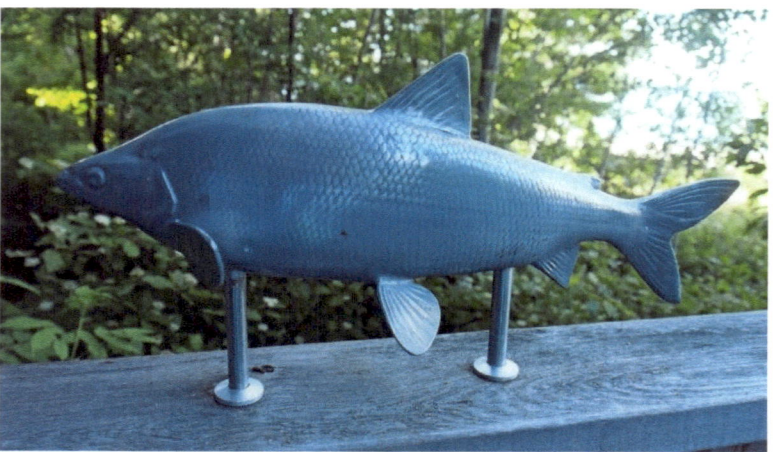

Lake Whitefish thrive in the cold waters of Lake Superior. They feed on the bottom on plankton and small invertebrates within a few miles of shore. In November and December, they spawn on reefs and shoals such as those around Lizard Islands.

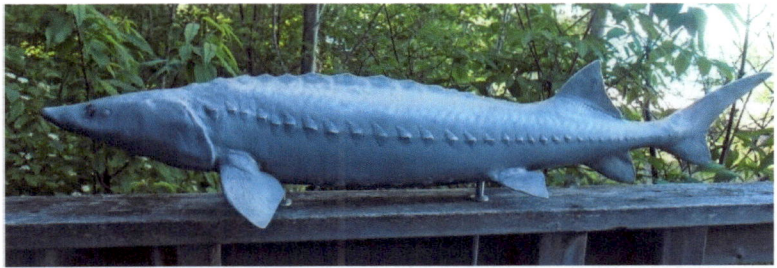

Lake Sturgeon use the whisker-like barbels around their mouths to feel for fish, crayfish, molluscs, insect larvae and vegetation on the bottom of the lake.

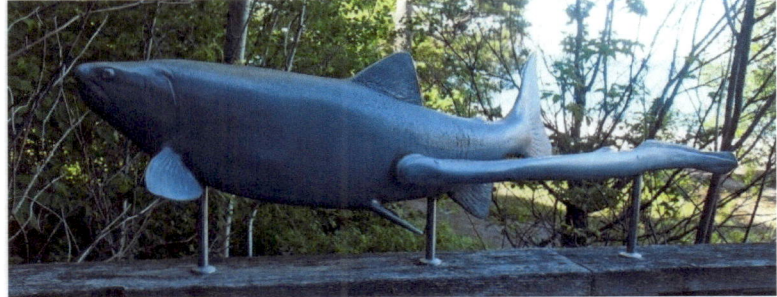

Lake Trout feed on smaller fish such as herring and whitefish. They spawn on rocky shoals from one to thirty meters (three to one hundred feet) deep.

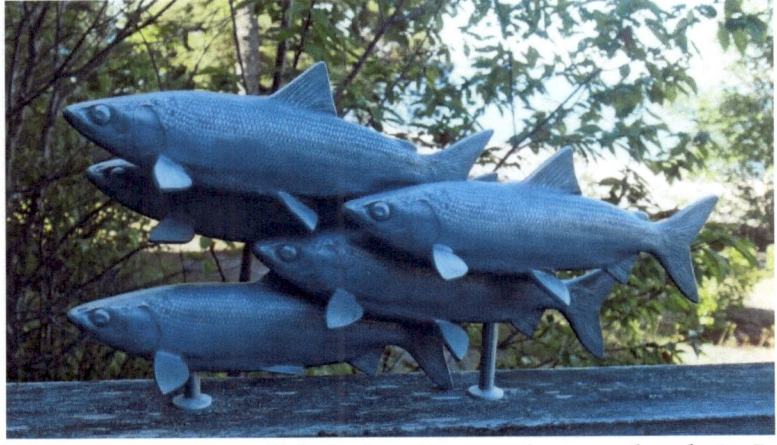

Lake Herring are small fish that live in dense schools in Lake Superior. The adults feed on plankton, crustaceans and insects.

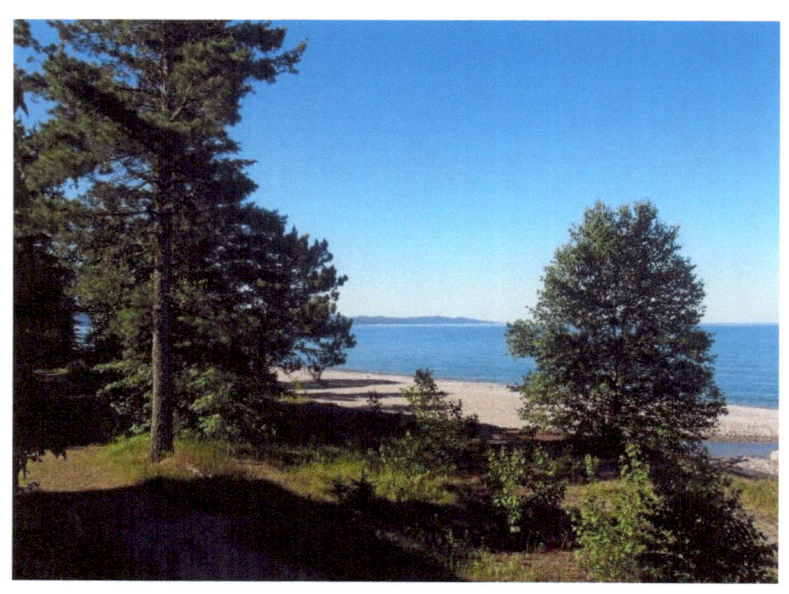

Lake Superior

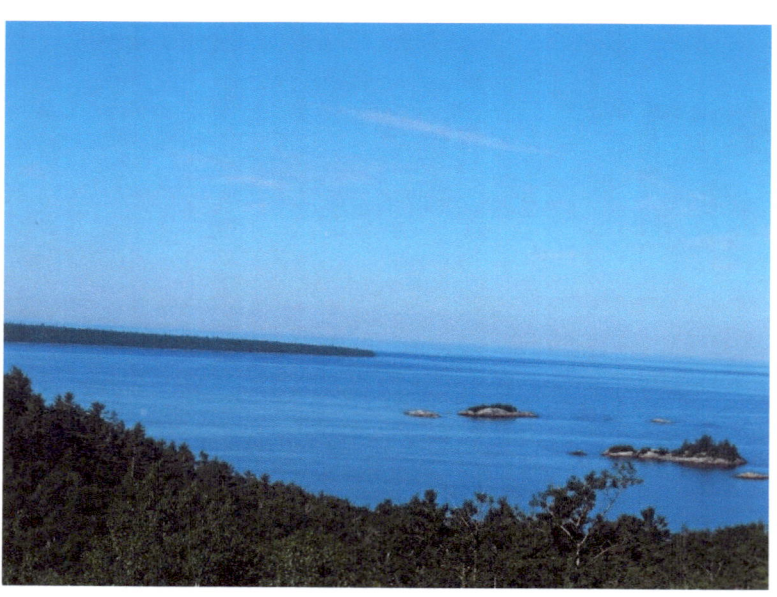

Pinguisibi

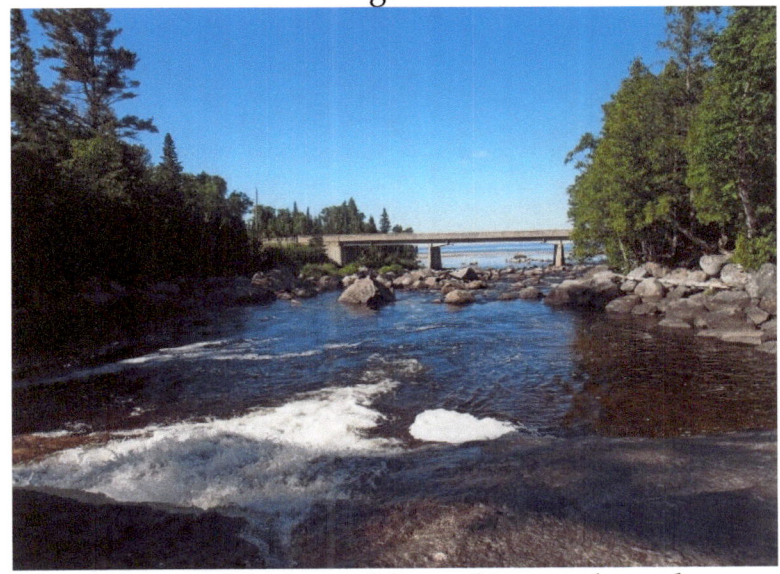

To the Ojibway, this river of fine white sand was known as Pinguisibi.

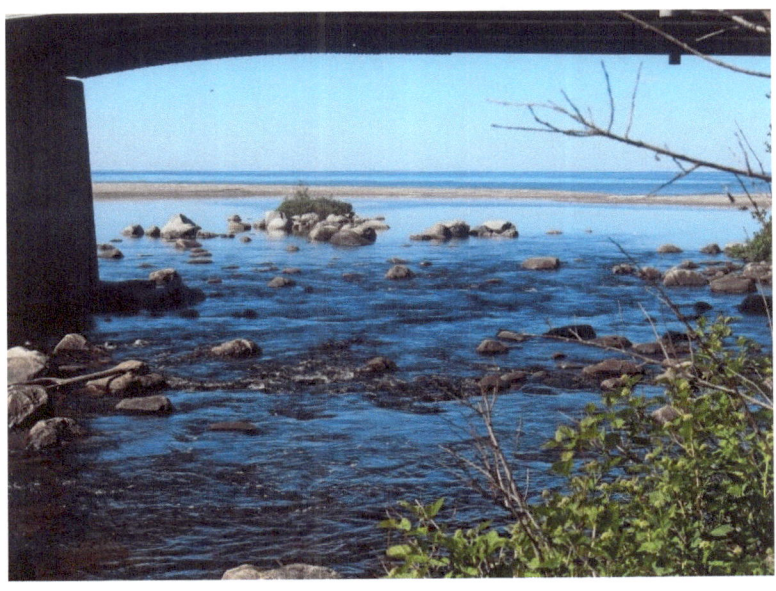

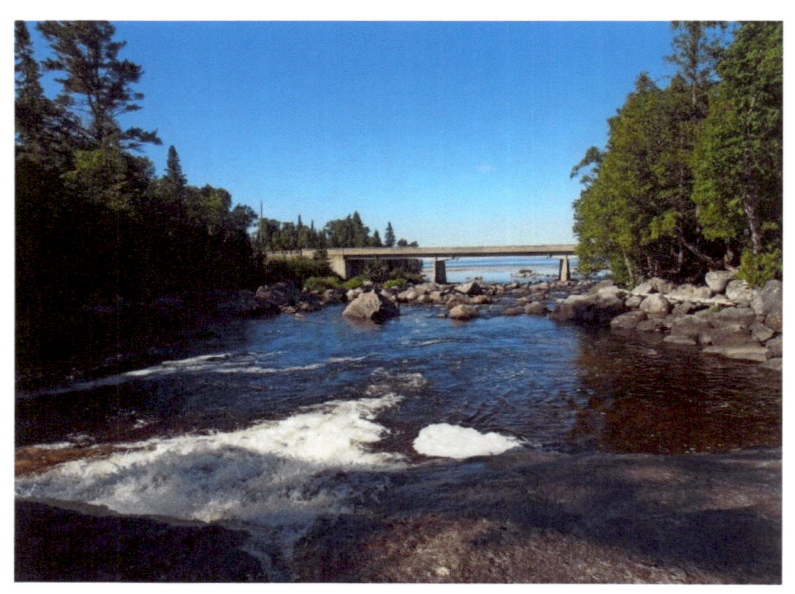

Katherine Cove

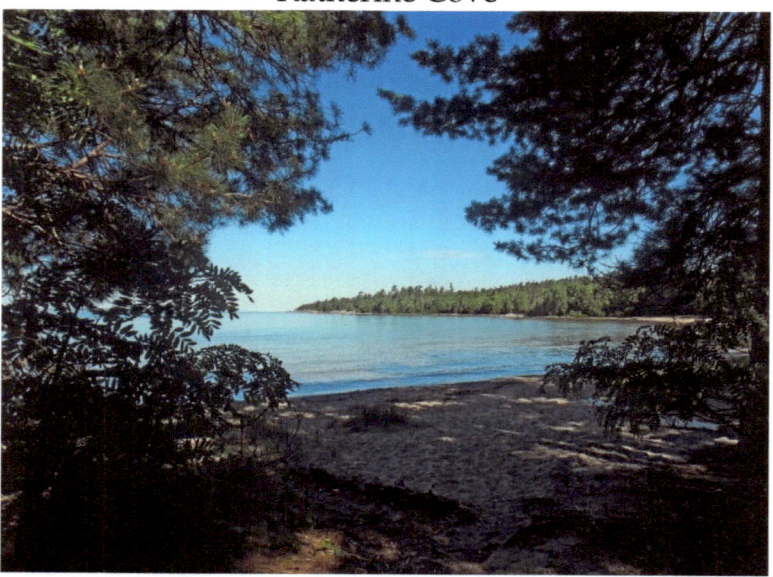

Here in the shelter of the Lizard Islands, the waters are warmer and shallower. The sand beaches of Katherine Cove are a great place for relaxing and having a picnic.

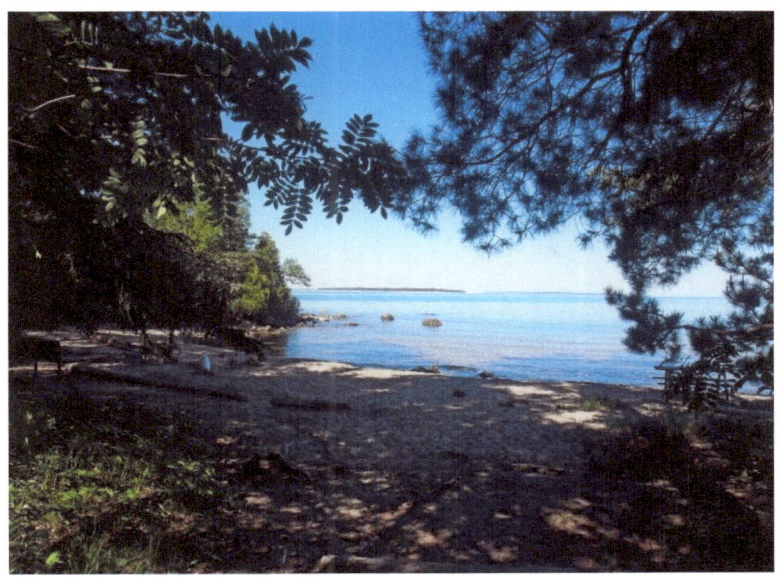

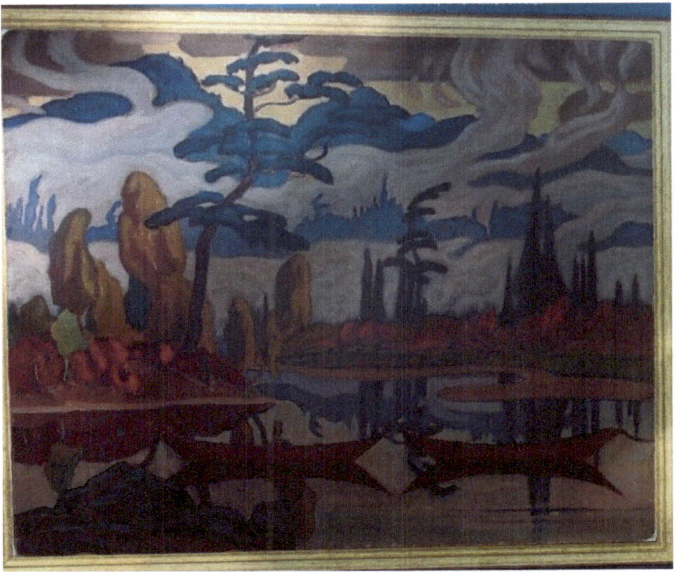

J.E.H. MacDonald's fanciful painting *The Spirit of Algoma* shows mists, water, reflections, and exotic canoes which create an image of Canadian Shangri La. Katherine Cove is the kind of place that inspired this theme.

Old Woman Bay

Formidable cliffs, forested hills and deep blue waters are the elements that define Lake Superior Provincial Park. At Old Woman Bay you can savour the awe and majesty of Lake Superior that inspired artists such as the film maker Bill Mason. In the cliffs, the face of an old woman looks out over the bay. This is a prime breeding ground for the fastest bird in the world, the Peregrine Falcon. They like to nest on the cliff ledges. Here their chicks are safe and from the cliffs peregrines can spy ducks and other birds which are their prey.

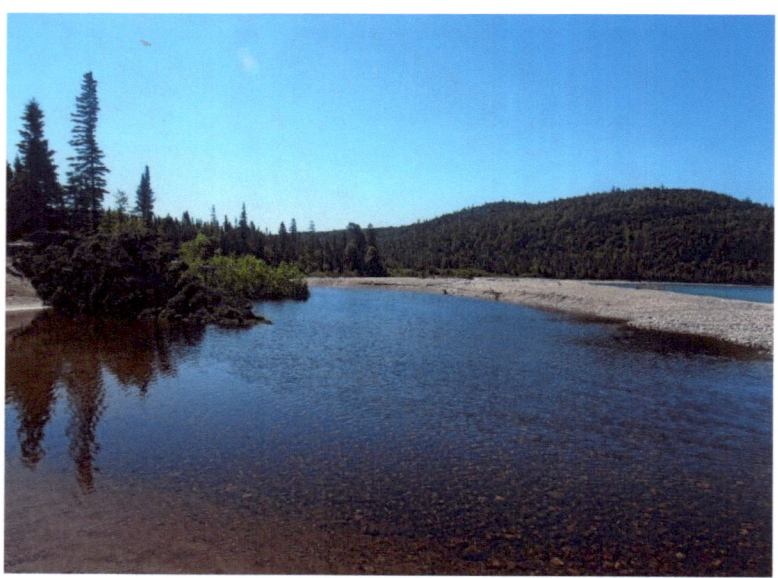

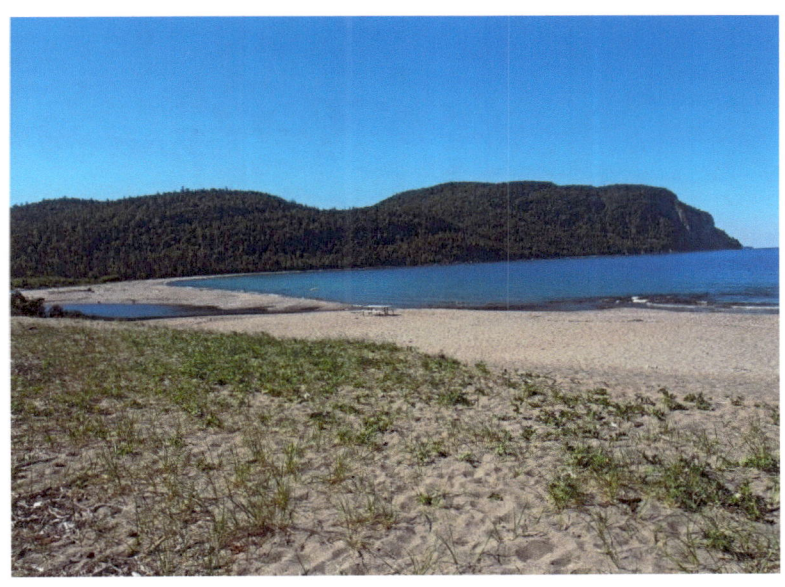

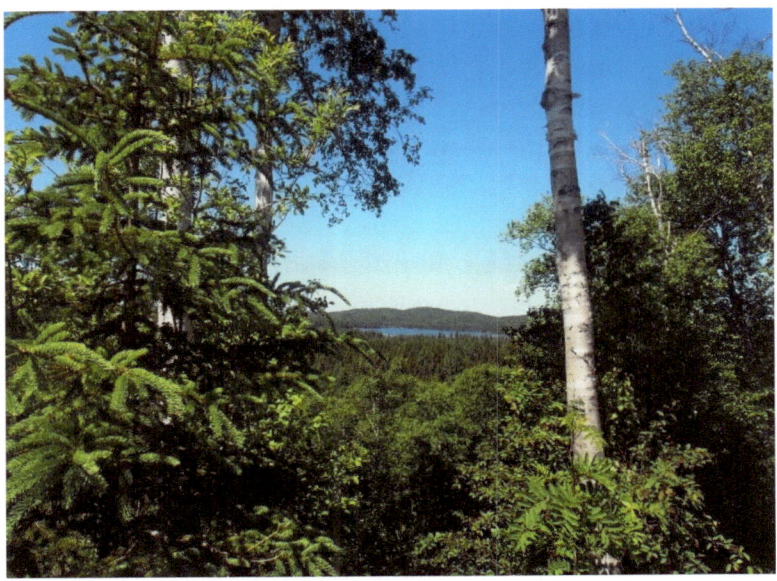

Wawa view

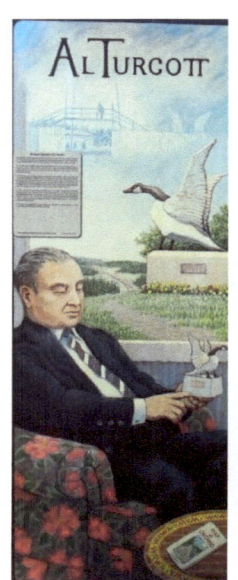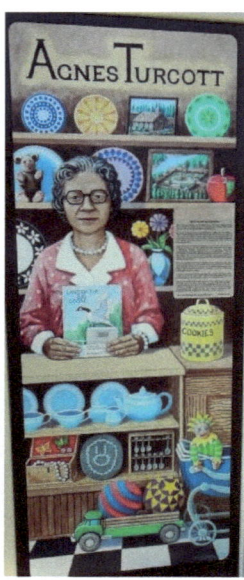

Born in 1907, Bernard Alphonse (Al) Turcott came to Wawa in 1939 expecting to be employed for six months with the construction of the crushing plant at the New Helen Mine. He liked the area and sent for his wife Agnes and two sons to join him. They operated Turcott's Dry Goods and Clothing Store. Both Al and Agnes were community minded people and they promoted the town. Al and a group of businessmen came up with the idea of the Wawa Goose statue as a tourist attraction. The first Wawa Goose statue was unveiled on September 17, 1960 at the opening of the last link of the Ontario and Lake Superior section of the Trans-Canada Highway. In 1969 the Turcotts proudly opened Fort Friendship, an imitation fort constructed on the banks of the Michipicoten River not far upstream from the original location of the two hundred year old Hudson's Bay Company post. This popular tourist attraction had log palisade walls, a museum, gift shop, wishing well, tower of Prime Ministers and a small church made out of glass bottles.

Agnes was the first town historian.

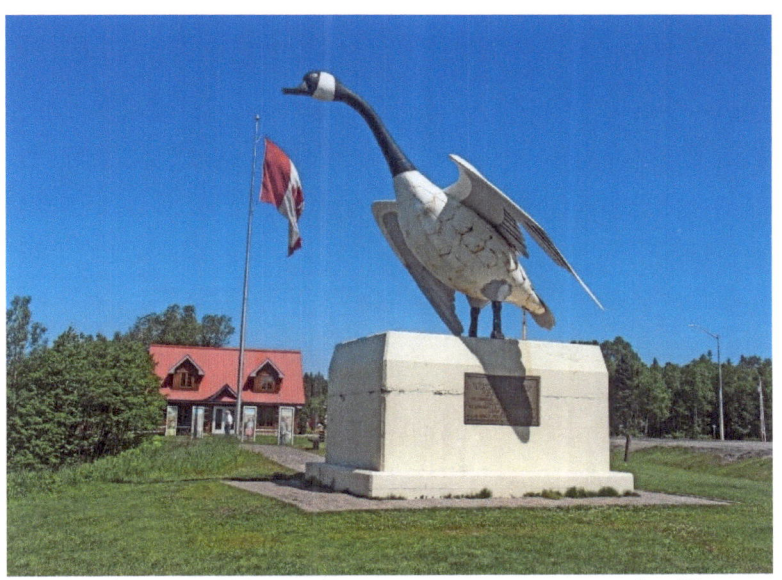

The famous Wawa Goose gazes out over the Trans-Canada Highway as it carries traffic through the Magpie River Valley. The Magpie River travels about one hundred and thirty kilometers over a number of scenic waterfalls (Steephill Falls, Magpie High Falls, and Silver Falls) until it merges with the Michipicoten River half a kilometer from its mouth on Lake Superior.

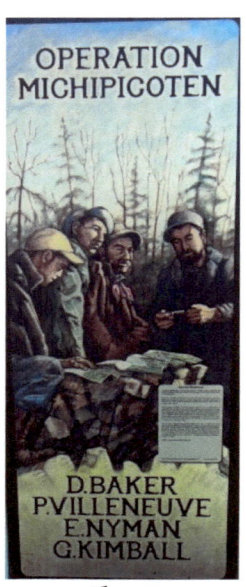

Operation Michipicoten was the name given to a project inspired by frustrated residents of the Town of Wawa who were eager for road access to their remote mining community. Prior to World War II in 1939, the Trans-Canada Highway had been blasted and cut out of the east shore of Lake Superior from Sault Ste. Marie north to Montreal River. At the bottom of the impressive Agawa River Valley is where it came to a halt for nearly twenty years. In 1951 residents of Wawa set out to make headlines and raise public awareness about the plight of Wawa. They set out to prove that if they could walk the sixty miles of the shoreline surely a construction crew could build a road. The highway was finally completed on September 17, 1960.

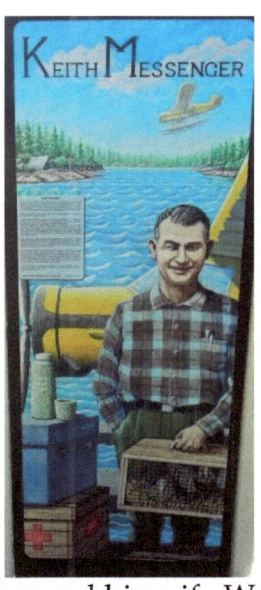

In 1948 Keith Messenger and his wife Wanda and their children moved to Algoma Mills with a DeHaviland Foxmoth and Fairchild 71 and started Great Northern Skyways. In 1949 they moved to Sault Ste. Marie with a Norseman and Cessna 180 and formed Sault Airways. Keith Messenger provided a scheduled mail service between Wawa and Sault Ste. Marie on a daily basis. The Norseman had pontoons and landed on Wawa Lake until the airstrip was completed. By the time the highway was completed in 1960, Keith was making up to five round trips a day between the Sault, Wawa and all points in between. Along with Wawa's mail and supplies, Keith's Norseman was a lifeline for residents who required emergency medical treatment in the Sault and beyond.

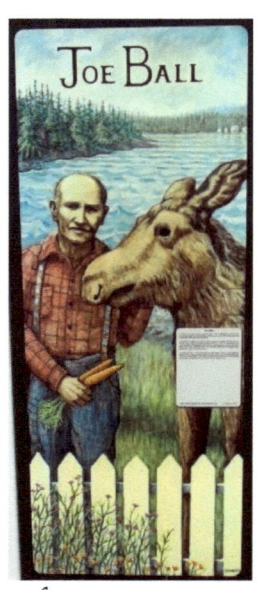

Joe Ball was one of many prospectors who was attracted to the lure of gold in the rugged hills around Wawa at the end of the nineteenth century. Joe worked as a caretaker at the Norwalk Mine, a gold mine located on Norwalk Lake. Later Joe worked at the hydro operations at Michipicoten High Falls.

Joe played the fiddle, cut and sold pulpwood, and trapped. He had a pet moose, a calf that had been abandoned by its mother, and which Joe adopted and raised.

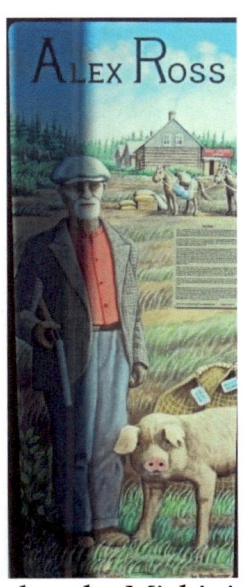

Alex Ross was attracted to the Michipicoten area after the cry of gold echoed through the hills in 1897. He first worked as a cook at the Minto Mine, then at the Ganley and Loyda Mines in the Wawa Gold Fields south of Wawa Lake. After the gold fever died down, Alex decided to call Wawa his permanent home. He helped build the town's first churches, and one-room school. Over the years Alex raised chickens and pigs for the locals and provided contractors and laborers with teams of work horses for all of their hauling needs throughout the area. The first Wawa Post Office was set up in his home.

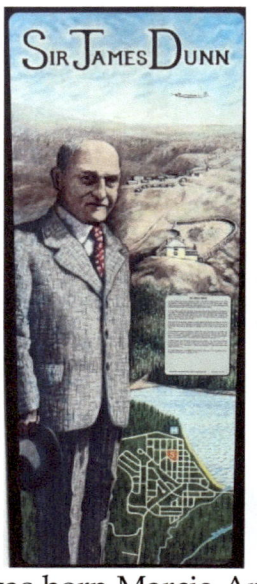 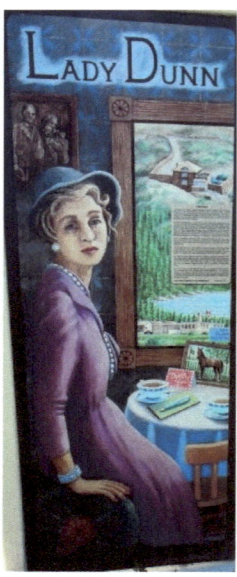

Lady Dunn was born Marcia Anastasia Christoforides in Sutton, England in 1909. During the Second World War, she became the personal secretary for Sir James Dunn, a wealthy Canadian financier who was responsible for the rebirth and development of the Helen Mine in Wawa and the Algoma Steel Corporation in Sault Ste. Marie in 1939. In 1942 Marcia and James were married. The Dunns had homes in England, France, and St. Andrews, New Brunswick. In 1945 they had a small house built for themselves at the top of the Helen Mine Mountain. It was named the "Eagle's Nest" and has a commanding view of Wawa, Wawa Lake, the Magpie River Valley, and Lake Superior in the distance.

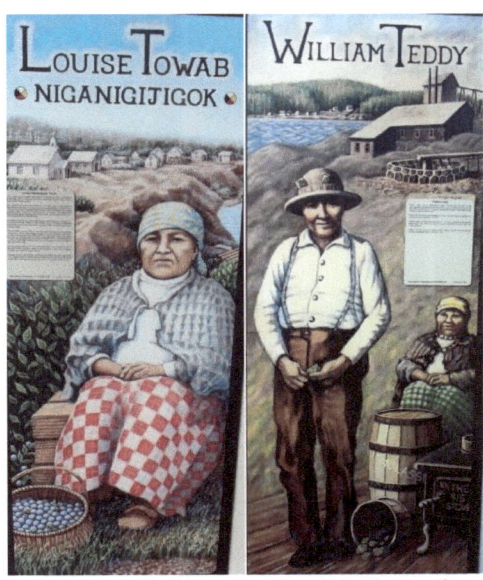

Louise (Niganigijigok) Towab

William Teddy was an Ojibway/Cree native Canadian born in 1855 in the Missinabie/Moose River region of northern Ontario. He worked as a guide for tourists, recreational fishermen, and prospectors travelling through the Michipicoten and Chapleau regions. William married Louise (Niganigijigok) Towab in 1878. Seven of their children died in an epidemic in 1895-96. William's legacy is the gold discovery which he and Louise uncovered on the shores of Wawa Lake in 1897. He was paid $500 for his claim. William was known for his kindly manners and generous nature.

The Miners' Story

The mineral rich mountains have brought men and women from around the world seeking their fortune in copper, silver, gold, iron, and recently in diamonds. The Ojibway mined a red mineral along Lake Superior's shore to make ochre, a special paint used in sacred rock painting. The heart of Wawa's mining history is the Helen Mine which opened in 1899 atop the largest hill that dwarfs the town. The mine closed in 1998.

At the beginning of World War II, Wawa's iron mine was the only iron producer in Canada.

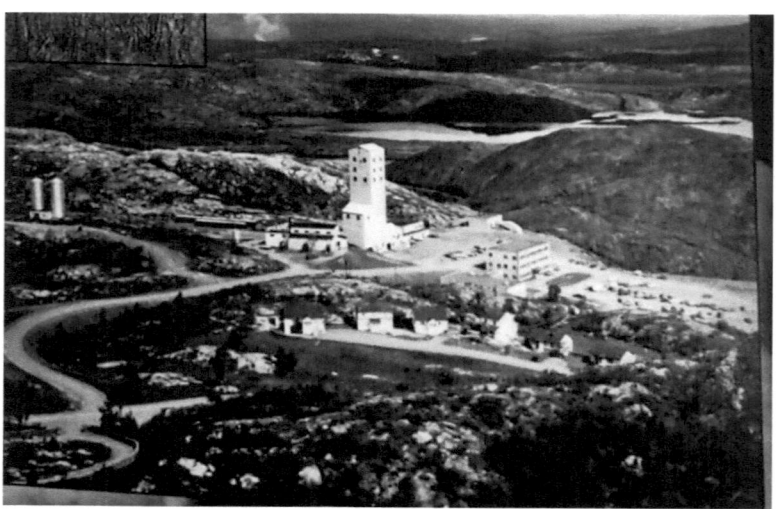

The Fisherman's Story

The lakes, rivers and streams of the Michipicoten region are a fisherman's dream. There are rainbow trout, lake trout, brown trout, brook trout, walleye, pike, sturgeon, smallmouth bass, yellow perch, whitefish, carp, chinook and pink salmon.

The Michipicoten Ojibway introduced the first fur traders to the abundance of fish which enjoyed the fertile river beds and spawning grounds in Superior's sheltered bays and inlets. The local Ojibway were employed by the Michipicoten trading posts to catch, salt and barrel fish for transportation to fish markets as far away as Chicago and Montreal.

Early residents living at the logging and mining camps depended on the "catch of the day" as a staple in their diets throughout the year.

Lake Superior

Lake Superior is what gives Wawa its unique character. The first lake vessels to travel the waterways were the fragile Ojibway birch bark canoes. The success of the early fur trade depended on them. To encourage larger loads and more profit, the Hudson's Bay Company built thirty foot wooden keel boats at the Michipicoten Post. To ensure safer docking for these boats and larger ones, a concrete wharf was built and two steamboats, the Caribou and the Manitou made trips twice a week from their home port of Owen Sound.

The need to ship iron ore to blast furnaces in Sault Ste. Marie led Francis Hector Clergue to give birth to the Algoma Central Steamship Line in 1899. Four English built steamships were the inaugural fleet of the longest continually operating Canadian bulk freight company shipping on the Canadian Great Lakes.

Pulpwood and lumber, passengers, fuel, sinter, coal, commercial fish and supplies were shipped in and out of Michipicoten Harbour from 1900 to 2000. Wawa's port had a school, hotel, general store, post office, boarding house, pool halls, and a customs officer. During World War II, Michipicoten Harbour was home to a POW camp which supplied labour on the pulp dock.

With the growing ship traffic and to ensure safe navigation in and out of the sheltered waters of Michipicoten Harbour, a lighthouse was built on Perkwakwia Point.

The Lumberjack's Story

Timber was the call of the lumberjacks as they cut white pine, jack pine, tamarack and spruce in the rugged river valleys of Michipicoten region. Wawa sits at the northern boundary of the Great Lakes St. Lawrence forests (maples, yellow birch and white pine) and the southern border of Canada's vast Boreal Forest (white birch, poplar, jack pine and spruce).

Small sawmills were a necessity for producing building materials at the Michipicoten trading posts, Michipicoten Harbour, and the many mining operations throughout the region. The construction of the Algoma Central Railway to Wawa required tamarack and spruce for railway ties, bridges and trestles. A pulp mill in Sault Ste. Marie led to the first harvesting of pulpwood along the Lake Superior shoreline and up the Michipicoten and Magpie Rivers. Pulpwood was cut in the winter and piled on frozen lakes. Fifteen dams were built between the upper streams of Mijinemungshing and the Michipicoten Rivers to ensure high water levels. During the spring breakup, the wood travelled downstream to the dams which were opened in a precise order to flush the logs down the rocky riverbeds to the Michipicoten River.

The wood was collected and gathered into large rafts. These log booms were towed by tugboats south to the pulp mills in Sault Ste. Marie.

The Native Story

Ojibway people congregated at the mouth of the Michipicoten River during the warmer months. The river was a natural transportation route and also provided an abundance of sturgeon, whitefish, and lake trout. Caribou, moose, bear and rabbit were hunted nearby. Berries were gathered in preparation for the colder months. During the winter, they divided into smaller family groups and headed inland. They depended on the forests for materials to build shelters and tools, for food, clothing and medicines.

Between 1725 and 1904, fur trading posts were found on both banks of the Michipicoten River a quarter mile from its mouth into Lake Superior. Birch bark canoes, keel boats, and supply ships travelled from here east to Montreal, west to Fort William, and north to Moose Factory.

The Railway Story

Michipicoten River Village was a supply depot for men, horses and supplies heading for the construction camps fifty miles east of Lake Superior. In the early 1880s, Mormon contractors for the Canadian Pacific Railway laid corduroy tote roads from Michipicoten Harbour and River to Wawa Lake and beyond. These tote roads are the foundation of many of Wawa's main routes. Some sections have been paved and become part of the Trans-Canada Highway, while other sections remain as gravel and show their original corduroy logs in the spring of the year.

When Francis Hector Clergue wanted to ship ore from Helen Mine in Wawa to his new steel mill in Sault Ste. Marie, he created the Algoma Central Railway in 1899. Ore, pulpwood, groceries and supplies, construction material, furniture, passengers and all their possessions were shipped on the railway. After the end of ferry service to Michipicoten in 1946, the railway was the only way in or out of the Wawa area until the completion of the Trans-Canada Highway in 1960. The train ride from Wawa to Sault Ste. Marie normally took eight hours. Rock slides, beaver dams, washouts, snow drifts, and moose caused slowdowns.

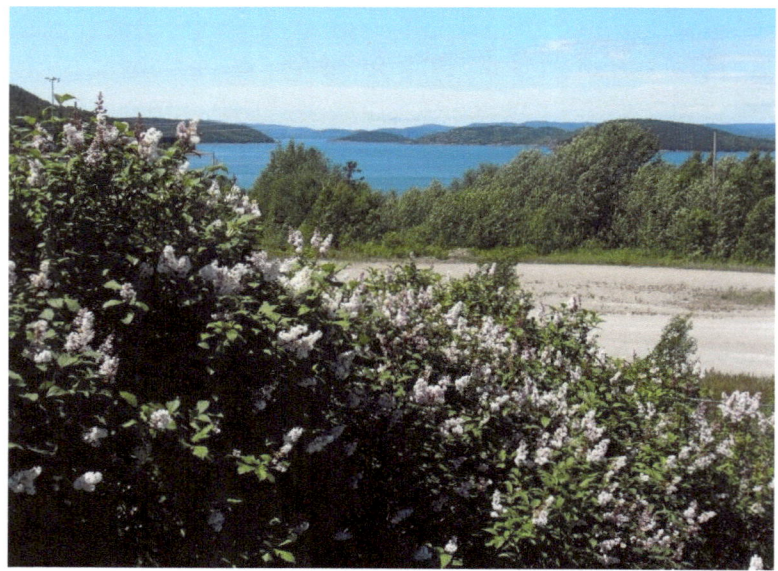

Marathon

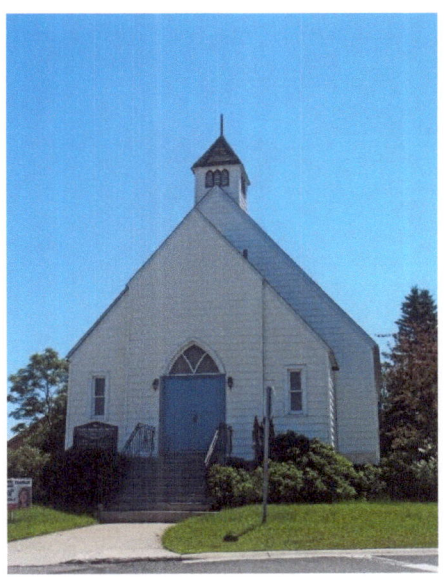

The Trinity Anglican Church, Marathon

Nipigon

The Canadian Pacific Railway came through Nipigon in 1885. The Canadian National Railway began construction through Nipigon in 1910. In order to complete the track with the least cost, the railway changed the course of the Nipigon River. The shoreline was extended by constructing a retaining wall and causeway which created the lagoon. The track work was completed by 1914.

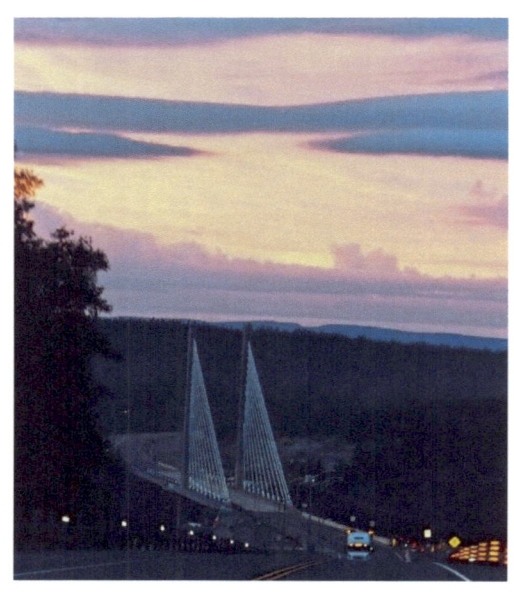

Nipigon Bridge at sunset

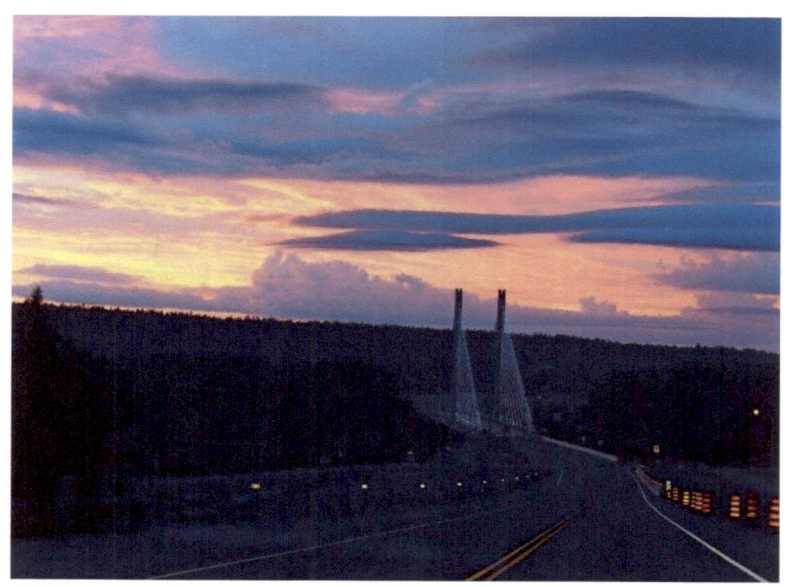

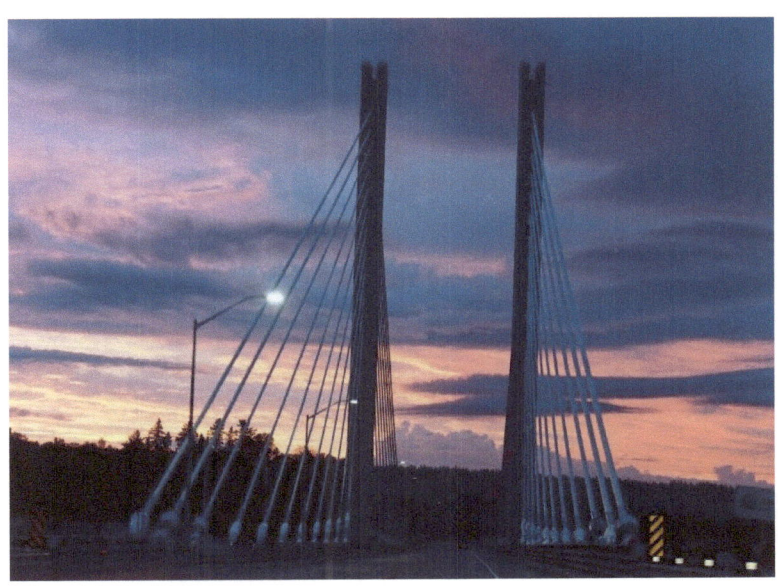

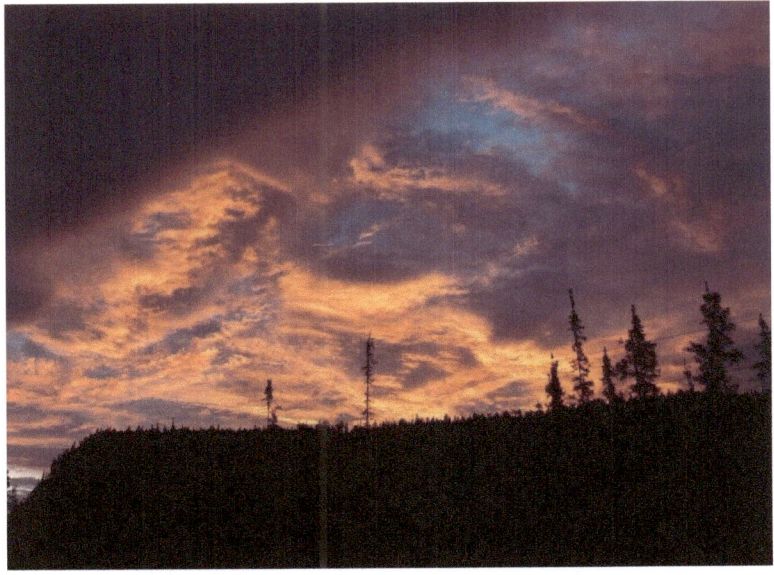

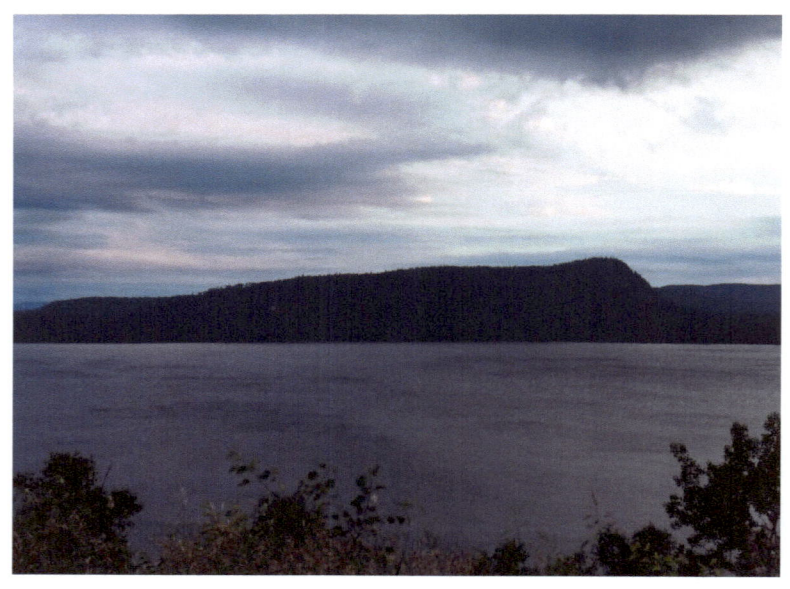

Lake Superior

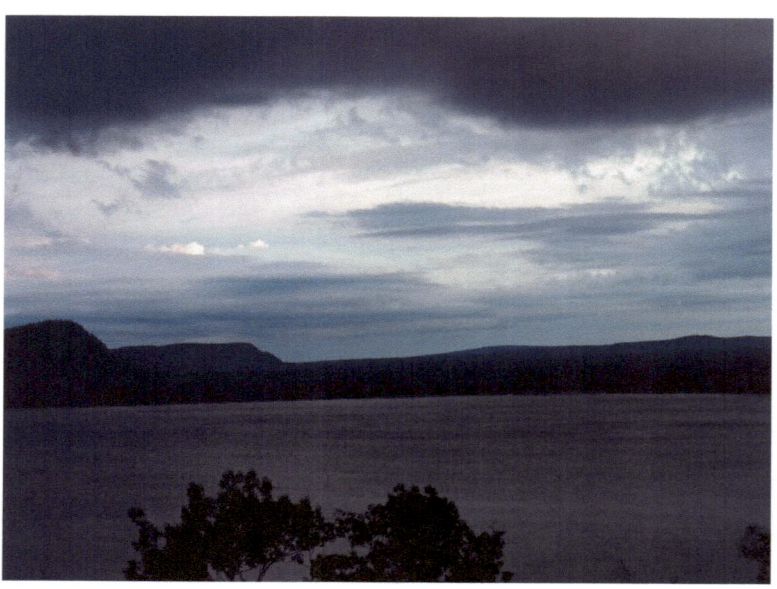

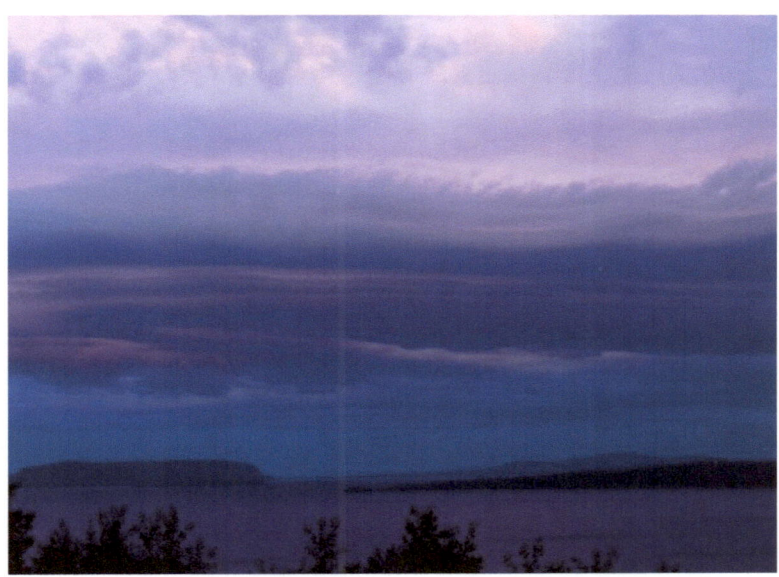

Just like a Group of Seven painting

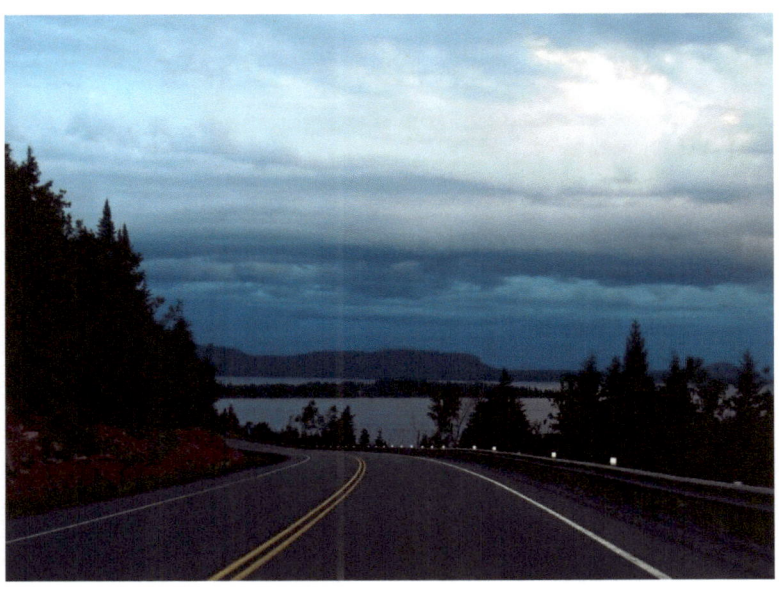

The Artic Watershed

   North of this watershed, all flowing water eventually reaches Hudson's Bay, while south of it all water courses form part of the Great Lakes drainage system.

North Woods

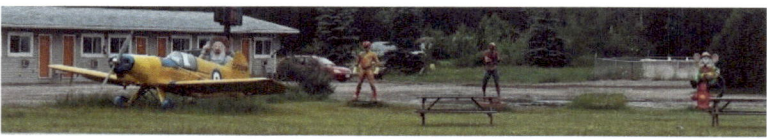

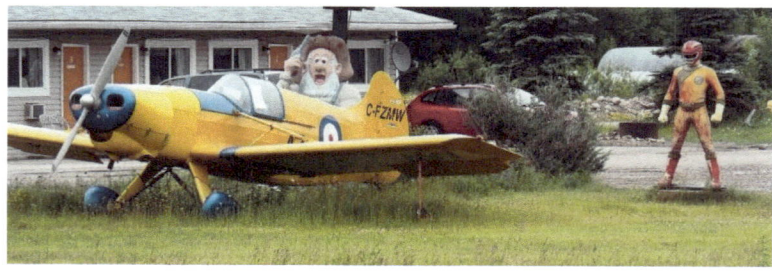

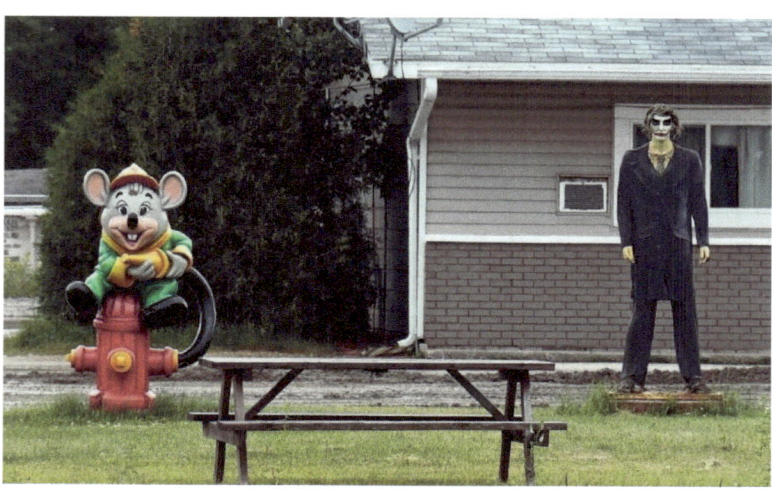

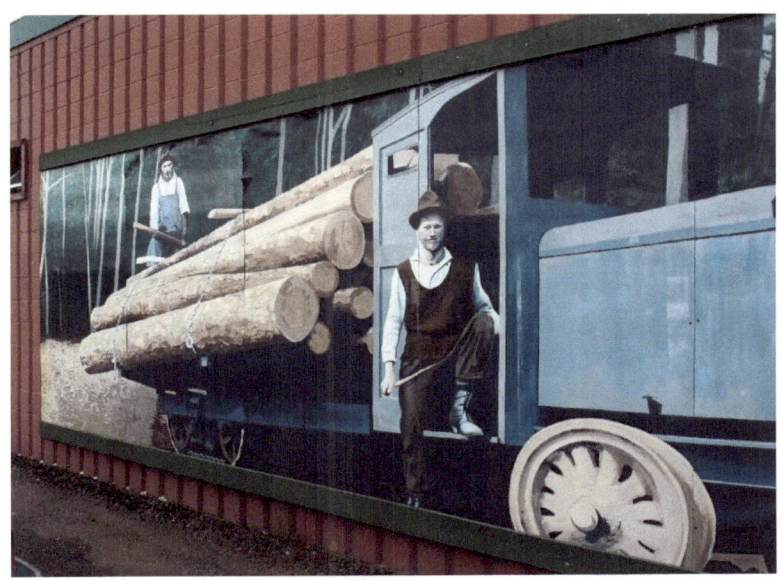

North Woods mural

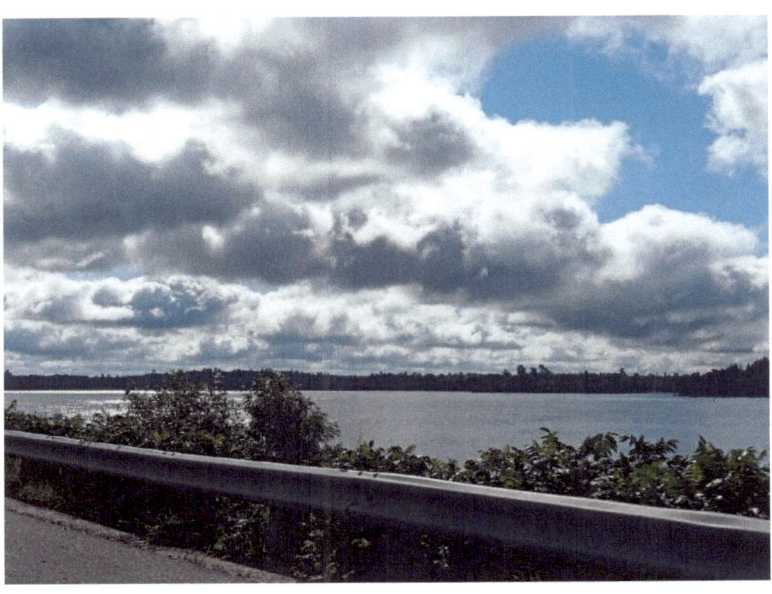

Kenora

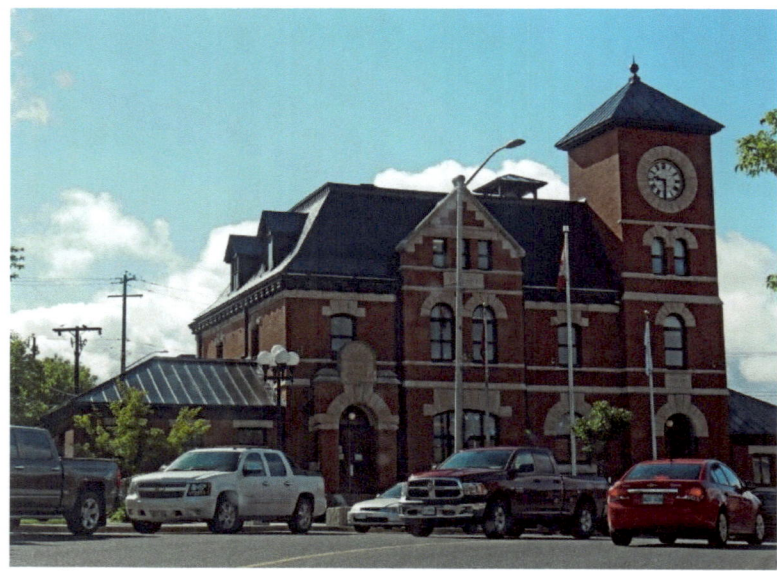

Post Office – A.D. 1898 – Second Empire style – mansard roof with dormers, dichromatic brickwork, banding, three-storey clock tower

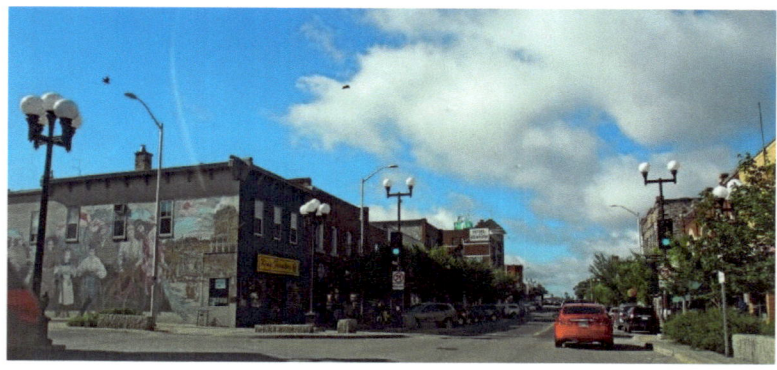

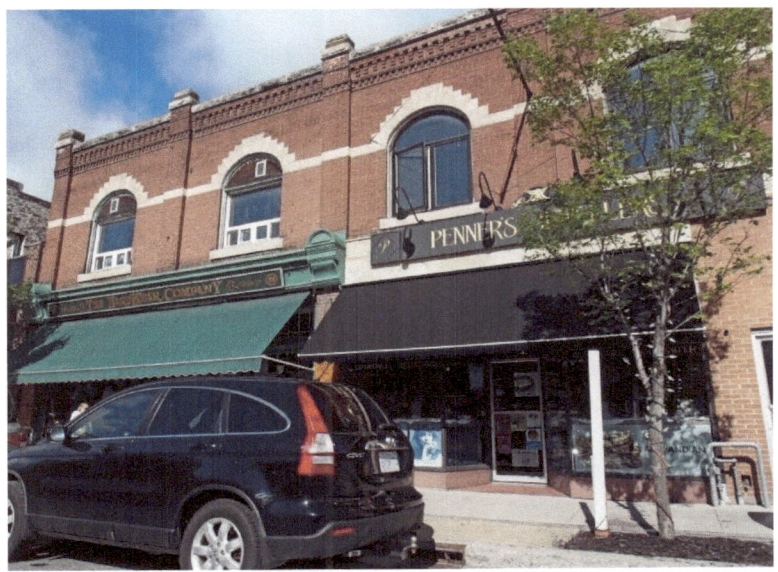

104-106 Main Street South - dichromatic brickwork, pilasters, banding, dentil molding

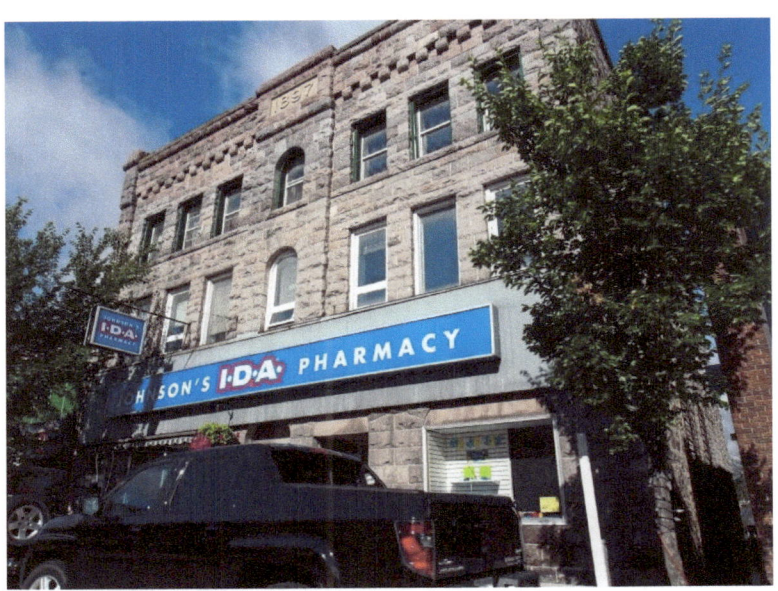

116 Main Street South - dentil molding - 1897

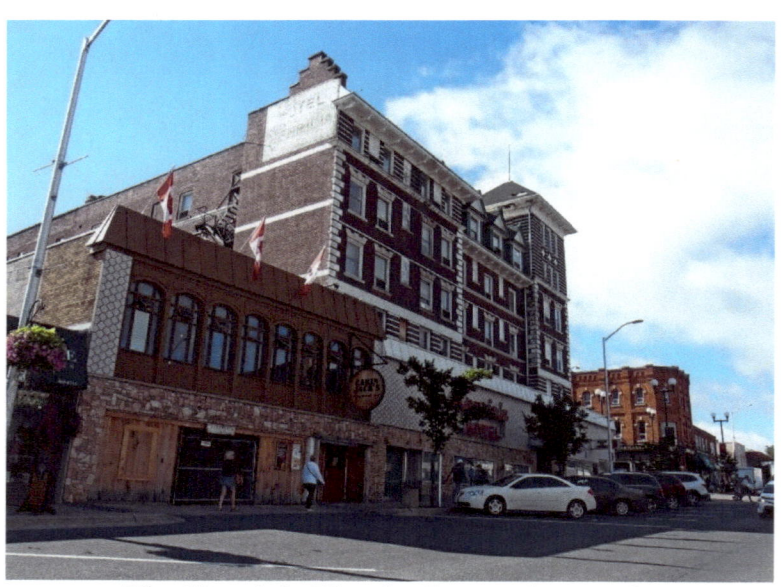

The Kenricia Hotel – Beaux Arts style

In 1907, Chicago architect Frank Newell was hired to design a hotel befitting the burgeoning tourist town. The Beaux-Arts style that Newell followed in designing the building was, in many ways, a reaction to Victorian frivolity and a return to classical traditions. The style is characterized by the pronounced limestone quoins along the corners of the building, symmetrical window hoods, the rectangular blocks (called modillions) edging the eaves, the symmetrical placement of windows, and the central projection of the tower.

The hotel was built of Wisconsin brick and limestone from Tyndall, Manitoba on the main corner of downtown Kenora Main and Second Streets South. It was completed in 1910.

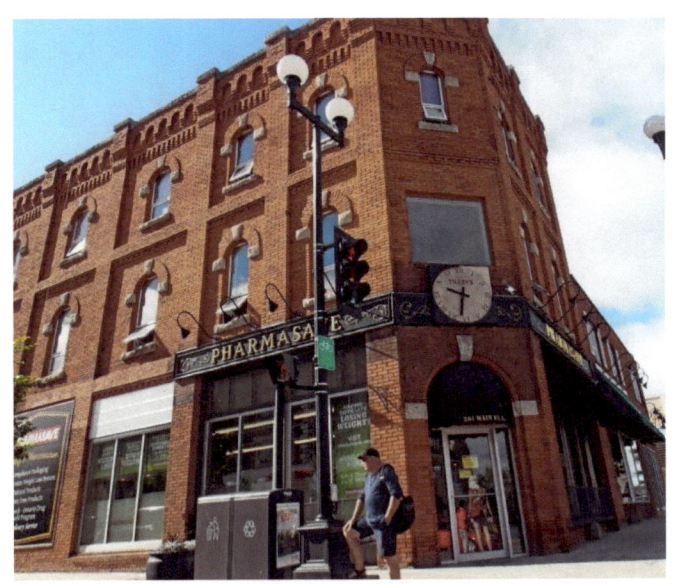

201 Main Street South, - dentil molding, pilasters, voussoirs and keystones

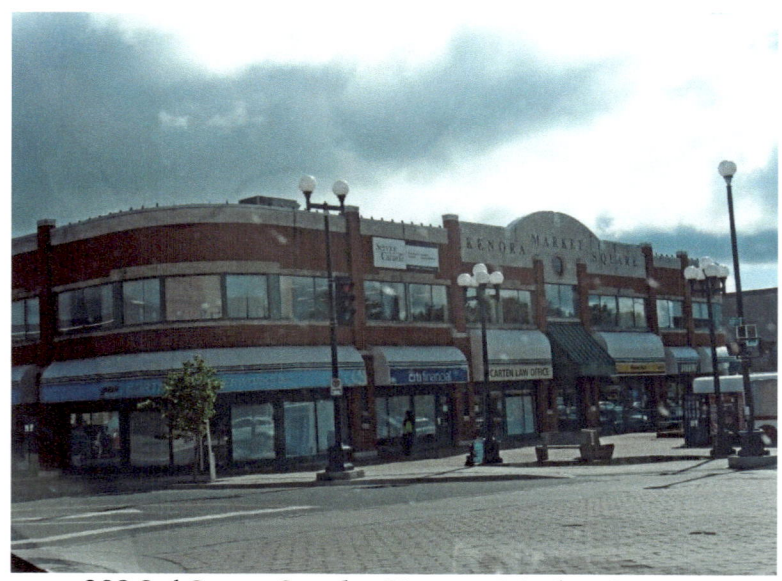

308 2nd Street South - Kenora Market Square

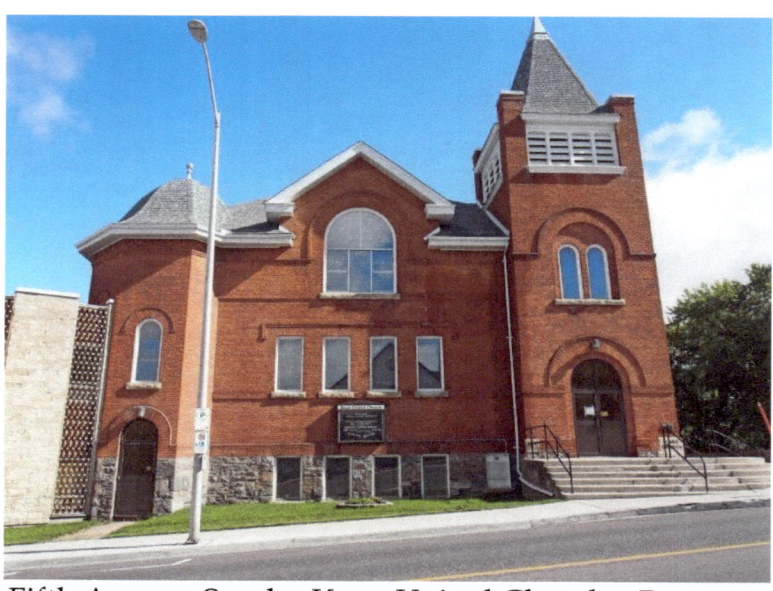

116 Fifth Avenue South - Knox United Church – Romanesque Revival style – cornice return on gable

Dryden

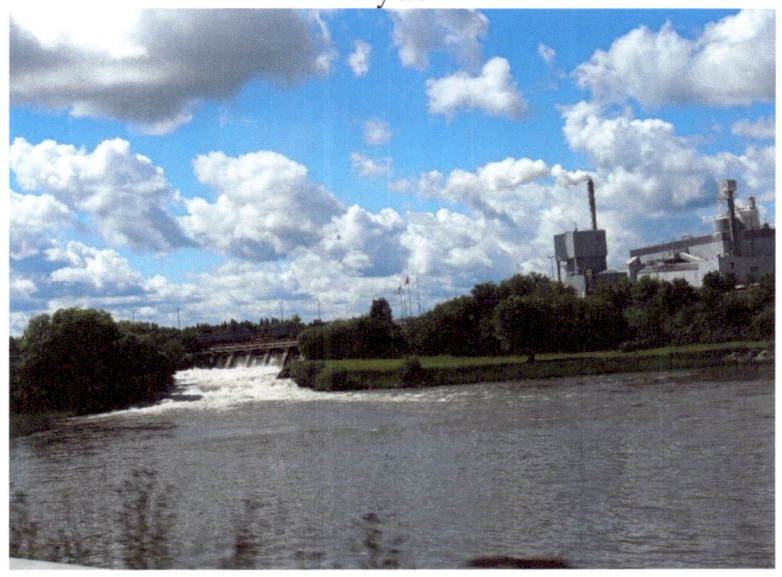

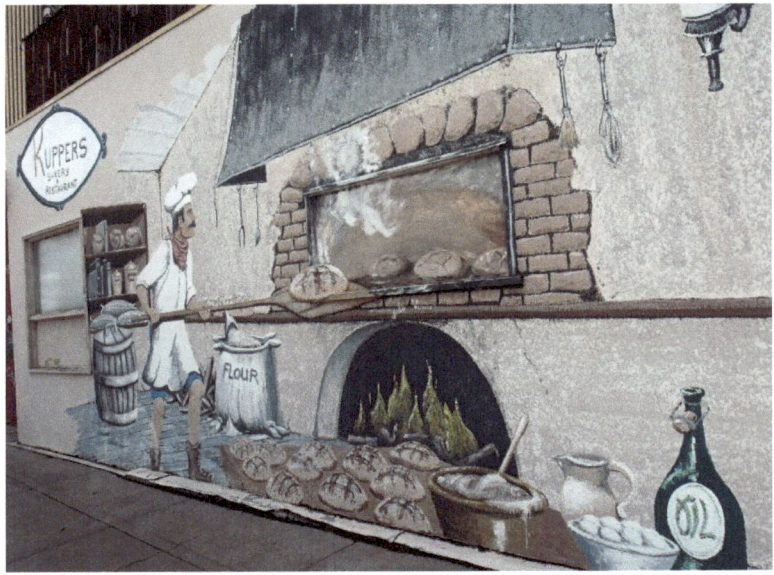

Kupper's Bakery and Restaurant - mural

1 Queen Street East (corner of Earl Avenue) – In 1897, M.C. Cassiday built a general store here. Alfred Pitt purchased the store in 1909 and enlarged it. After 38 years, Mr. Pitt retired and his son John operated it until 1954. Chapple's Limited of Fort William leased it until 1964 when George Kupper created Kupper's Bakery and Restaurant.

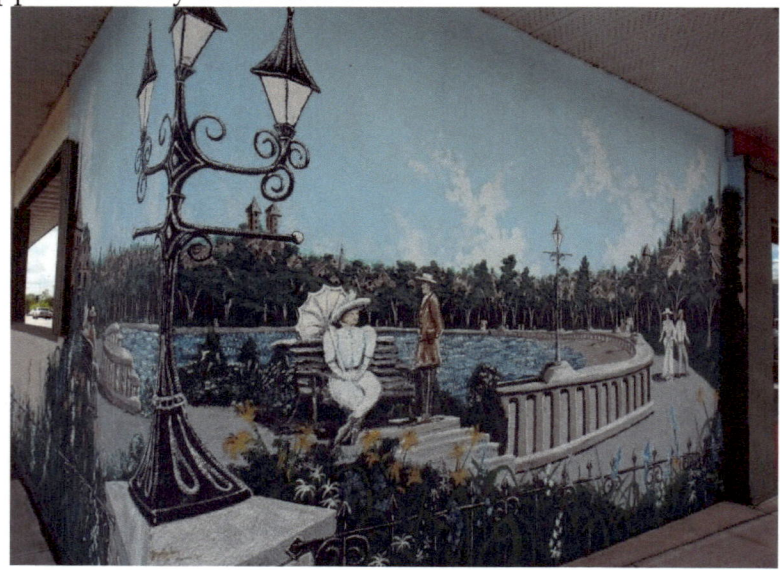
Mural

Alfred Pitt was born in England in 1871. By the time he was 16, he knew French, Flemish, Spanish, German and conversational Latin. He learned elementary mathematics, mythology, history, theology, and geography. He could play the piano and the pipe organ. When he came to Canada, he first settled in Manitoba; he moved his family to Dryden in 1909. In the store, Mr. Pitt sold everything from food and supplies to coal oil, and even bales of hay. Groceries, men's and boys' clothing and shoes were located on the main floor. Women's and children's clothes, kitchenware, household items, rugs and furniture were on the second floor.

Alfred Pitt was Dryden's first mayor, serving on and off for twenty-five years. Carrie, Alfred's wife, was born in Fort Frances in 1878; her father was a Methodist missionary to Native Americans.

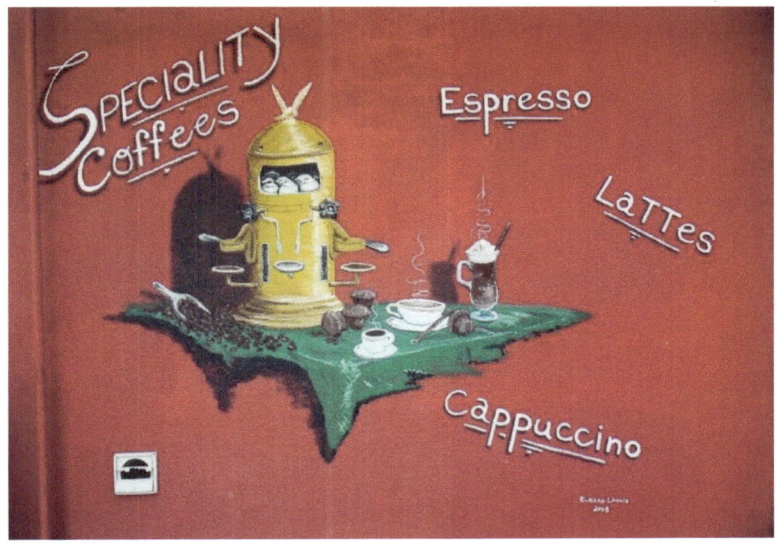

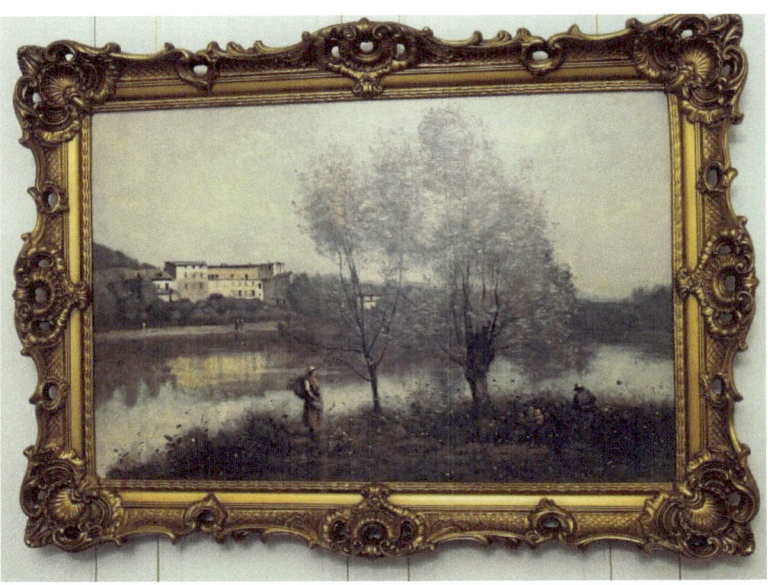

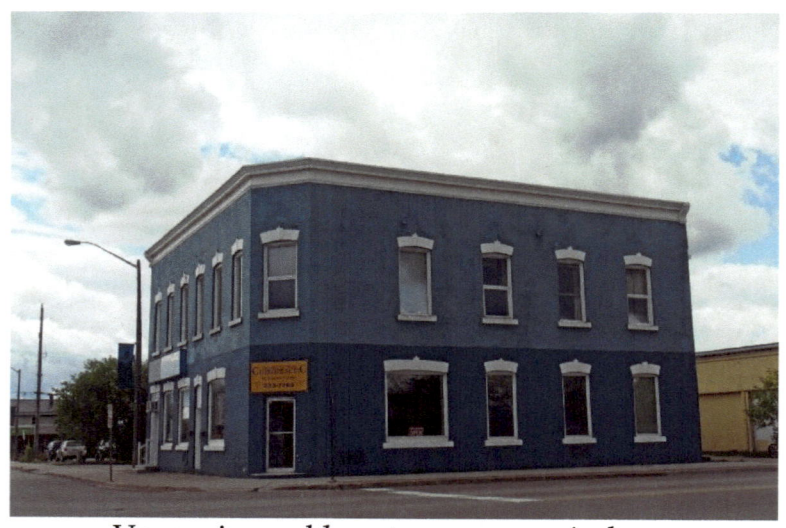
Voussoirs and keystones over windows

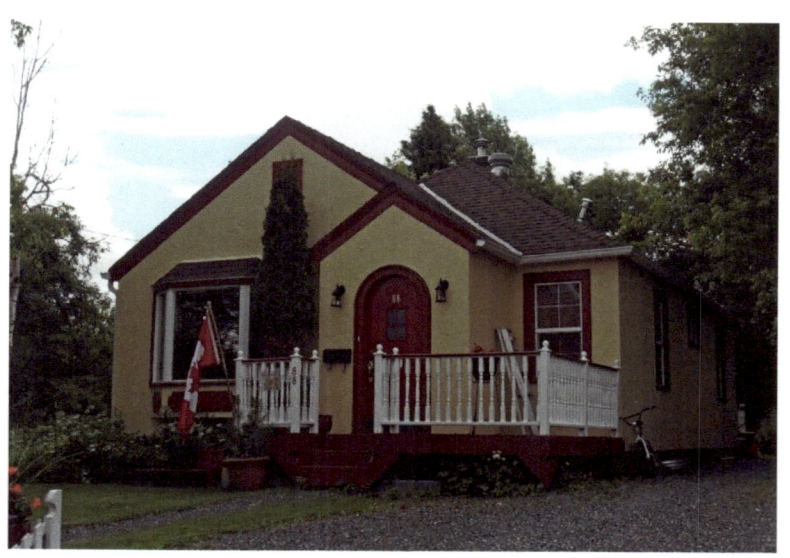

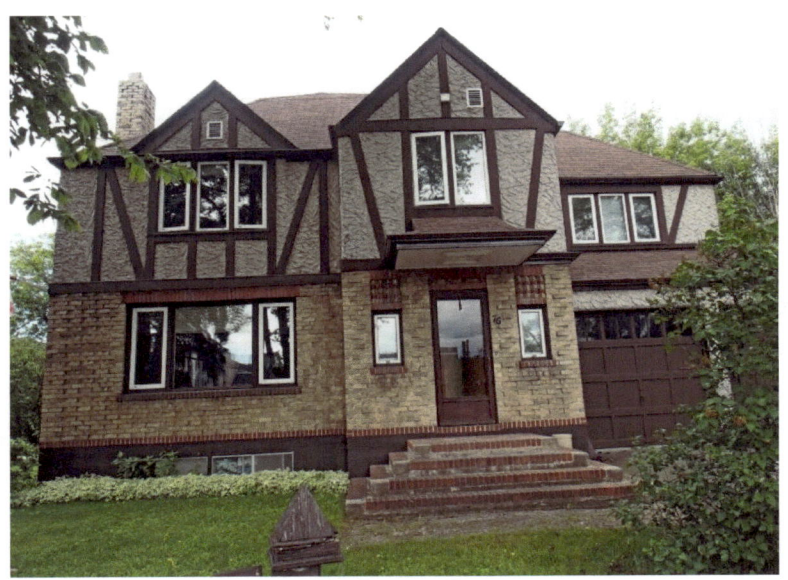

Tudor style

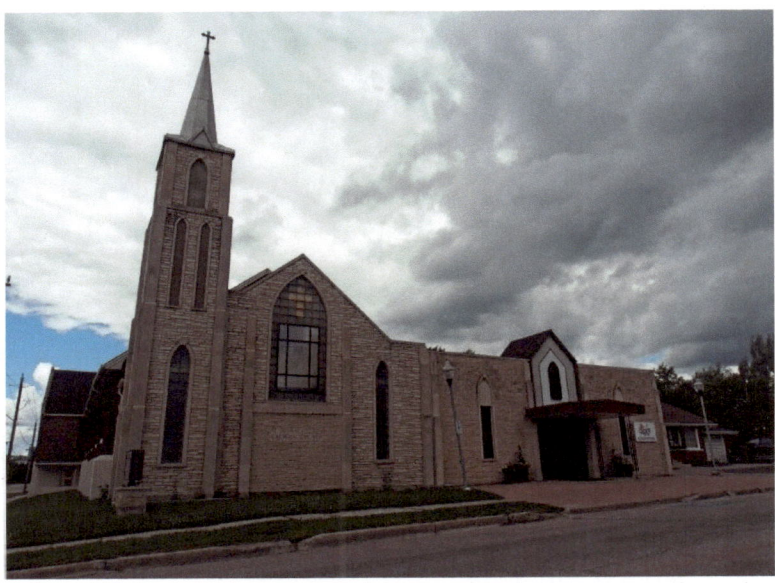

102 Van Horne Avenue - St. Joseph's Catholic Church – buttresses, lancet windows, three-storey tower with steeple

Architectural Terms

Buttress: a masonry structure built against or projecting from a wall which serves to support or reinforce the wall. In Canadian architecture, they are sometimes used for decoration. Example: 102 Van Horne Avenue, Dryden, Page 49	
Cornice Return: decorative element on the end of a gable. Example: 116 Fifth Avenue South, Kenora, Page 44	
Dentil Moulding: an even series of rectangles used as ornamental decoration in cornices. Example: 104-106 Main Street South, Kenora Page 41	
Dichromatic brickwork: the use of two colours of brick, tile or slate to decorate a façade. Example: Post Office, Kenora, Page 41	
Dormer: (French for "sleep") a gable end window that pierces through the plane of a sloping roof surface to create usable space in the top floor or attic of a building by adding headroom. Example: Post Office, Kenora, Page 41	
Gable: the triangular portion of a wall between the edges of a sloping roof. Example: Dryden, Page 50, top	

Keystones and Voussoirs: a voussoir is a wedge-shaped element used in building an arch. A keystone is the central stone that locks all the stones into position, allowing the arch to bear weight. A keystone is often enlarged and embellished. Example: 201 Main Street South, Kenora, Page 43	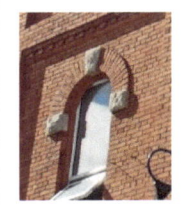
Lancet Window: a tall, narrow window with a pointed arch at its top. Example: 102 Van Horne Avenue, Dryden, Page 49	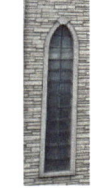
Pilaster: a slightly projecting column built into or applied to the face of a wall for additional structural support. Example: 201 Main Street South, Kenora, Page 43	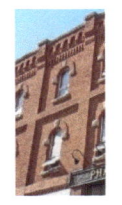
Tower: A circular, square, or octagonal vertical structure higher than the surrounding structure that is usually part of an existing building and is created either for extra defense or for a specific purpose such as a clock or a bell tower. Example: Post Office, Kenora, Page 41	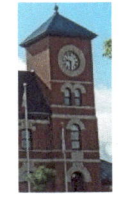

Building Styles

Beaux Arts: Promoters of this style sought to express the classical principles on a grand and imposing scale. Many of the Beaux Arts buildings were banks, post offices, and railway stations. The Ontario Beaux Arts style is eclectic mixing elements of Classical, Renaissance and Baroque. Often the designs have a temple-like façade, porticos with pediments, balustrades, and capitals in many styles. Example: The Kenricia Hotel, Kenora, Page 42	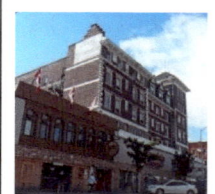
Romanesque Revival, 1880-1910 – This style hearkens back to medieval architecture of the 11th and 12th centuries with a heavy appearance, blocky towers and rounded arches. Example: 116 Fifth Avenue South, Kenora, Page 44	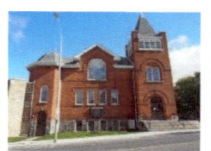
Second Empire, 1860-1880 – The mansard roof is the most noteworthy feature of this style and is evidence of the French origins. Projecting central towers and one or two-storey bays can also be present. Example: Post Office, Kenora, Page 41	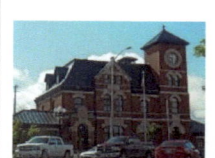
Tudor Revival – exposed timbers with stucco infill, multi-paned windows. Example: Dryden, Page 50, Top	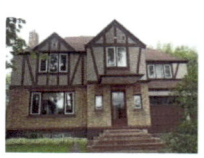

www.ingramcontent.com/pod-product-compliance
Lightning Source LLC
Chambersburg PA
CBHW040243220526
45473CB00001B/355